A Guide to the Eskimos and Inuits

An illustrated introduction to the art, clothing and life of the Eskimo and Inuit peoples

by Sarah Byers

Cover image credit: P J Hansen

Introduction

This little book offers an insight into how the Eskimo and Inuit peoples lived in centuries gone by. Although their unique way of life has been lost in many places as tribal communities become more integrated with Western customs, many of the traditions depicted in this book still exist on some scale. Igloos are still built, fish still caught with harpoons, and many neighboring tribes each with their own identities still communicate. Many tribes still struggle with their identity in modern times, with many fondly remembering the old traditions of hunting and community.

I hope that you, the curious reader, enjoy learning and seeing how the tribes of the Arctic lived.

- *Sarah Byers, Spring 2016*

Table of Contents

The Laughing People 6

Inventions Old and New 9

Papik and his Clothes.. 11

Inside the Igloo 13

Breakfast is ready 17

Getting Ready for a Trip 19

Papik Hunts Seal 22

A Use for Everything 26

Building a Snow Igloo 27

Summer is coming 34

Eskimos Made Wonderful Inventions 41

The Eskimos Share What They Have 46

Mackenzie Eskimos... 49

Using New Things 52

New Ways and Old 53

They Didn't Get Lost 55

Fooling the Seals.. 57

Fish to Eat 59

Open Water 62

Neighbors 63

Greenlanders.. 65

Trouble Ahead 68

Eskimo Cowboys 72

The Eskimo ABCs 73

Doctors, Nurses and Medical Help 74

Dancing and Air 75

The Laughing People

If you could look down at the world from high above the North Pole, this is what you would see—an icy ocean with land almost all around it. The brown-skinned people who have lived along this shore for many hundreds of years are Eskimos. The shaded areas upon this map of the Arctic Circle show where the Eskimo peoples have settled.

This shows all the places where Eskimos have lived.

A harpoon brings smiles to the people's faces

When white men first met the Eskimos, they were surprised by several things. The Eskimos never used salt. They lived on nothing but meat and fish and water. And they were the most cheerful people in the world. An Eskimo laughed more in a day than anyone else did in a week.

Nobody knows exactly where these laughing people came from but many scientists think they traveled across from Siberia into Alaska, just as their cousins the Indians did. Nobody knows why they decided to stay there near the top of the world. But we do know that Eskimos like the country where they live. They settled along the shore of the ocean where they could find both sea and land animals to eat. The weather there was not as cold as it was farther inland or even in some parts of the United States.

Long ago Eskimos invented wonderful ways of getting food and of staying warm. They trained dogs to pull their sleds. They learned to find their way home over great fields of drifted snow, even in the dark night. They knew exactly what to do in order to live and have a good time.

Papik with his fish spear

The Eskimo people found different ways of living in different parts of the Arctic country. But everywhere they had many of the same customs. Some groups settled near forests, and they used wood in their tools and for building igloos. (Igloo is the Eskimo word for house, no matter what it is made of.) Other groups had no trees, so they made skin tents for summer and snow houses for winter, and they used bone and ivory for tools. One group lived where they could find chunks of pure copper which they made into tools. A very few learned to make tools from the iron in meteorites. (A meteorite is a shooting star that has landed on the earth.)

Inventions Old and New

When white men moved into the Arctic country, Eskimos borrowed many modern inventions, such as guns and stoves, and they changed many of their old ways of living.

A salmon hook

Although their tools and things are simple, the Eskimos still think they are luckier than people who live where houses are big and hard to build and the hot summers are long.

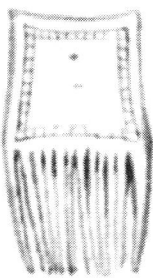

An ivory comb

Summer in Eskimo land is often hot, but it's always short. For several weeks the sun shines night and day. Winter lasts for more than half of every year up there, and for several weeks the sun doesn't shine at all—it's dark night twenty-four hours a day.

A great many customs in the warmer parts of the world seem strange and silly to the Eskimos. They think they do things the way people should naturally do them. In fact, they call themselves The People.

The fringe of land where The People spend their lives belongs to different countries now. Part of it belongs to the United States, part to Canada and Denmark and Russia. But The People are still Eskimos. They all talk the Eskimo language wherever they live.

Their language is one of the hardest in the world to learn. In order to speak it, you must know many more words than most people ever learn in order to speak English. In the old days Eskimos had no alphabet and no way of writing down their language. But today many of them can read and write, and there are even books and newspapers in Eskimo.

Papik and his Clothes

A long time ago, an Eskimo boy named Papik lived in a tiny village on Baffin Island. All winter his home was a round little house built of snow, out on top of the frozen sea.

Papik was warm and comfortable in his snow house, and outdoors he kept warm, too. He looked all bundled up in his clothes made of animal skins, but his winter suit was really lighter and softer than yours.

Papik wore these clothes in winter. His mother sewed good luck charms into them.

It was easy for Papik to get dressed. First he pulled on his pants made of baby sealskin, with the soft, white hair on the inside. Next he put on his deerskin stockings and his slippers of bird-skin with the feathers inside. Over these he drew a second slipper of sealskin and his waterproof sealskin boots.

Finally Papik slipped his jacket over his head. He even had his cap on because it was made right into his jacket.

Papik didn't have to fuss with buttons or zippers. He just tied an animal-skin around each leg to hold the tops of his boots up. Now he was dressed in his underclothes—which were also his summer outfit.

His mother's jacket was extra-large so she could carry his baby brother inside it on her back.

To go outdoors in winter, he put on an extra pair of pants and an extra jacket made of deerskin with the hair outside. These, with deerskin boots and mittens, were all the clothes he needed for a trip out over the ice with his father.

Each mitten looks as if it had two thumbs—and it had. Papik's mother made them that way so that he could turn them around without taking them off and wear them backwards if he got one side wet.

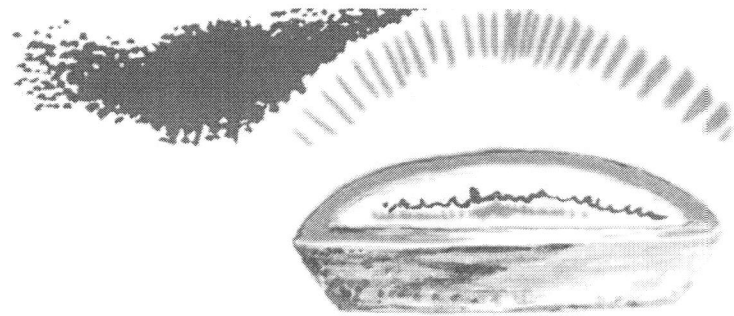

Eskimos lit their lamps by striking sparks from stones called flint and pyrite.

Papik's sister Milak wore clothes almost exactly like his. The grownups did, too. When white men came to the Arctic, they found Eskimo clothes were better for winter there than anything else that could be made.

Inside the Igloo

Papik and Milak had no regular bedtime. They slept when they were sleepy. Lamps burned in their house all the time to give heat as well as light.

An Eskimo lamp worked in the cleverest kind of way. It was made of soapstone—a soft stone that could be hollowed out into a bowl. This bowl was filled with oil which came from seal fat, called blubber. Along one side of the bowl ran a little ridge of moss. This was the lamp's wick.

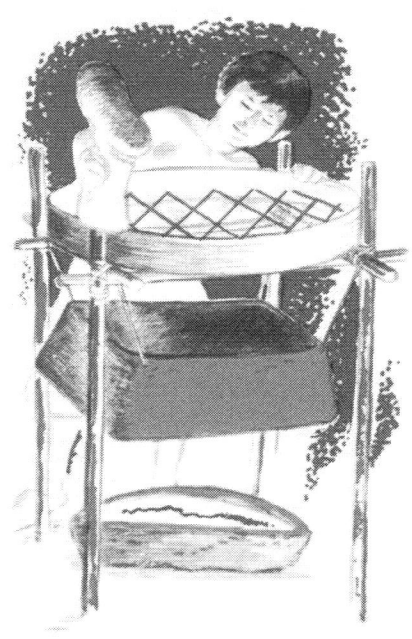

A cooking pot hung above the lamp. The rack was for drying clothes.

When the wick was lighted, it burned with a hot, white, steady flame. The children's mother watched it and was careful that it never smoked. To keep the lamp filled, she put a chunk of blubber near the flame. As the flame burned it kept melting oil out of the blubber, and the oil kept oozing down into the bowl where the wick soaked it up. The lamp never ran over and never ran dry.

Eskimos never scolded their children for waking them up.

Sometimes the round dome-shaped room got too hot and the roof began to melt. Then Papik would go out with his snow-cutting knife and help his father fix the drip. Instead of patching the roof, they shaved it down! This made the ceiling colder, and the dripping water froze. When the house was not warm enough, Papik and his father went out and heaped more snow on the roof and sides. This kept the cold out.

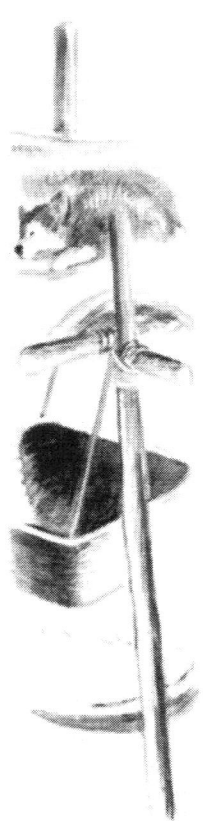

Sometimes new puppies were kept warm in the rack over the lamp.

The seal oil lamp was also a cooking stove. When Milak and her mother wanted to cook, they hung a soapstone pot over the flame. They melted ice and snow for drinking water in a pot, too. Some of the ocean ice was too salty for drinking water. But many Eskimos knew that when ice was a year or more old it lost its saltiness, and that was the ice they melted.

Milak didn't have to help with much cooking. Eskimo families on Baffin Island liked meat and fish raw. In fact, that is where the word Eskimo came from. It was the name that the Indians gave to their neighbors in the north, and it meant "People-who-eat-their-food-raw."

An Inuit fork

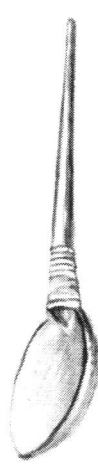

An Inuit spoon

Before breakfast time, Milak went outside and got a chunk of frozen fish. The whole outdoors in winter was a deep-freeze, so it was easy to keep a good supply of food. Milak tossed the fish on the floor. When it had thawed till it was about as soft as cream cheese, her mother cut off the best chunks for the children. Grownups didn't start to eat till the children had been served.

In winter it was breakfast time whenever anybody woke up and began chattering to the others. Because it was so dark outside in the long winter night, nobody kept track of time. Eskimo families just slept and woke when they felt like it.

Even when it was quite dark Papik sometimes went hunting with his father. First they got their sled ready. The sled was made of bone and pieces of driftwood, with a high pair of deer antlers for handles at the back. Its runners had to be slick and smooth so that the dogs could pull it easily.

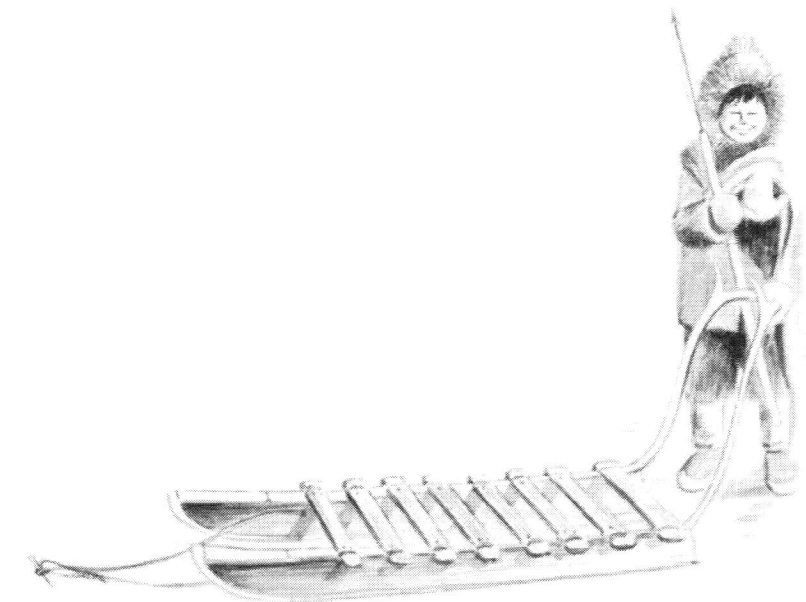

Eskimos had different kinds of sleds. This was Papik's.

Long ago the Eskimos discovered that a coating of ice made a sled's runners good and slick. But ice won't stick very well to bare wood or bone. So this is what they did: At the beginning of winter they plastered the runners with a thick coat of mud and decayed

19

moss, which would stick tight when it was frozen. Now an ice coating would stick to the mud.

Hunters riding on sleds never talked to each other, because if they did the dogs would stop and listen.

Each time Papik used the sled, he iced the runners. He filled his mouth with water and squirted it back and forth. As the water froze, Papik squirted on more, until he had a thick layer of ice over the mud and moss.

Next Papik and his father put harness on the dogs and hitched each one separately to the sled. While the dogs barked and quarreled with each other, Papik hung a snow knife and a rope made of skin over the sled's handles. He put a harpoon and a big polar bearskin on the bottom of the sled, and now they were ready to start.

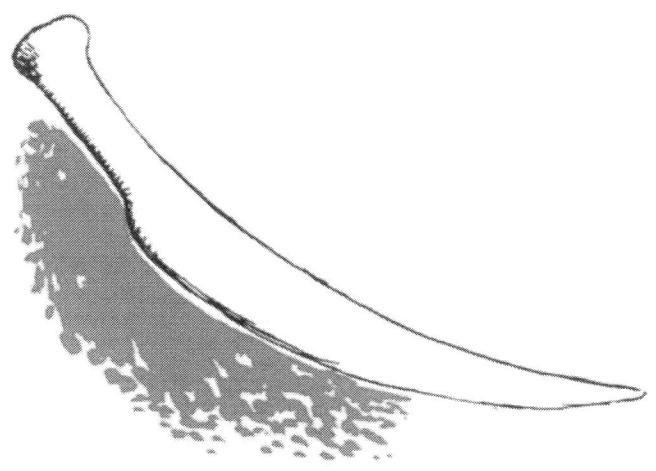

A snow knife made of walrus ivory for cutting snow.

Papik's father snapped his long whip over the dogs' heads. He could make the whip crack right near a dog's ear without ever touching it. Papik could do this, too. By the time he was six years old, he could aim the whip anywhere he wanted to, although the lash was more than twenty feet long.

At the whip's crack, the sled was off. The team spread out like a fan behind the lead dog, who was a natural leader and always traveled at the very front. Papik sat on the bearskin behind his father who used the whip to guide the dogs.

At a place where they thought there might be seals, Papik and his father stopped.

They turned the sled upside down and pushed the points of the runners and the antlers deep into the snow. The sled had to be an anchor to hold the dogs while the Eskimos hunted. Now Papik unhitched the lead dog and held tight to his harness strap. The dog ran ahead, sniffing the snow. He was looking for a seal hole.

Although seals lived in the water, they weren't like fish. They had to come up for air. When the ocean froze, they gnawed many breathing holes through the ice. They could get plenty of air through the holes, even when a blanket of snow covered the ice.

The harpoon handle came loose from the barb.

The sharp barb of the harpoon acted like a fishhook.

The hunter held on to a line attached to the barb and pulled the harpoon handle out, so it would not break.

Suddenly the lead dog began to bark. He had smelled a seal hole. Papik pulled him away and ran back to the sled. He must not let the dog frighten the seal away.

Papik's father poked around in the snow till he found exactly where the hole was. Then, with his snow knife, he carved a snow seat so he could be comfortable while he waited for the seal to come. He put a piece of fur under his feet with the hair side up. He might have to wait motionless for hours, and he had to keep his feet warm. Beside him he laid his harpoon—a special kind of spear with a line attached to it.

For a long time Papik played near the sled. At last his father's sharp ears caught a little noise. It was a seal breathing. Quietly he stood up, plunged his harpoon straight down, and hit the seal.

A woman's knife was called an ulo.

Papik came running at his father's shout. Together they chipped the ice away from the edges of the hole, making it big enough so they could pull the seal out and kill it.

Milak's doll is made from materials gathered during the hunt.

Now they took little ivory pins and closed up the slit that the harpoon had made in the seal's skin. They didn't want any of the animal's blood to spill out. Seal blood was an important food. And when it was prepared in a special way, the children often used it for chewing gum, too! Papik's family, and the dogs as well, would have plenty to eat when they got home.

A Use for Everything

Milak and her mother were ready to cut up the seal with a special knife, called a woman's knife. They cut the blubber away and carefully peeled off the thin layer of skin between the blubber and the hide. When this thin skin was dry, they would use it like cellophane, for wrapping things.

Eskimo women did almost no cooking or housework so they had time for sewing the warm clothes everyone needed.

An ivory needle

A thimble to protect the sewer's finger

An Eskimo woman could do wonderful things with her hand-carved ivory needles and the thread made of animal tendons called sinew. She could join skins together so that they were absolutely watertight. As Milak and her mother worked, they sang. Milak made dolls out of scraps of fur.

When Papik and Milak weren't busy, they played outside in the snow with other children. They tumbled around with the puppies, threw snowballs and slid down their houses.

The houses were very strong. They could last all winter. But very often a family or a whole village would pack up and go off to find new hunting grounds or just to visit another village. When they moved, they built new houses, if they didn't find empty ones to use. It took only a few hours to make a new house. This is how Papik's family did it: His father looked for a place where the snow had drifted deep in one big storm, so that he could get solid, even chunks of it. Snow on level places in Eskimo land was seldom very deep!

With his snow knife Papik's father cut out blocks about the size and shape of a small suitcase and placed them in a circle ten or twelve feet across. Each block leaned inward.

The second row of ice blocks begins to spiral upward.

After the first row of blocks had been laid, Papik's father shaved two of them down, the way you see in the picture. When he laid the next row, the blocks began to slant in a spiral, upward and inward. Soon, the spiral almost closed in over his head, because he worked inside while his family worked outside.

This snow house would be used for hunting or a short visit. It had no window.

Finally, there was only a small hole at the very top. He cut a block just the shape of this hole and fitted it into place. Now he was inside a house that had no door!

But he and his wife had already decided where to put the door. So he started to dig his way out, making a tunnel under the wall. At the same time, his wife tunneled toward him from the outside. After a while they met. Now they made the tunnel strong by roofing it over with snow blocks.

A regular house had a window made of seal intestines sewed together. Or it might have a pane of thin clear ice.

Papik and Milak were busy all this time, too. They pushed loose snow into the cracks between the blocks. Then they helped shovel more snow all over the house and tunnel. When they were through, it looked just like a snowdrift.

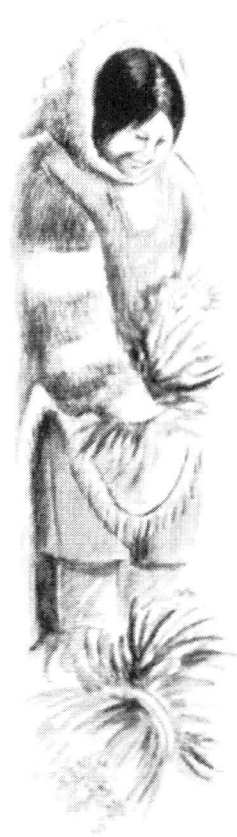

Unpacking dry heather for mattresses

Inside, their father cut a small hole up through the roof for ventilation. Cold air would come into the house through the tunnel. Hot air would leave through the hole in the roof.

Next, their father dug the middle of the floor deeper, leaving a snow bench all around the circular room. He tramped hard on the floor to pack it down. Then he sprinkled water on it to give it a hard finish.

Milak and her mother were ready to make the beds. They unpacked bundles of dry heather—a plant with tough, springy stems—that they had collected in the summer. They spread the heather on the snow benches. This was a mattress. Over it they laid deerskins, making one big blanket for the family.

The snow benches were seats as well as beds. Often Papik and Milak sat there cross-legged, while their parents made tools and clothes or sang or told long stories.

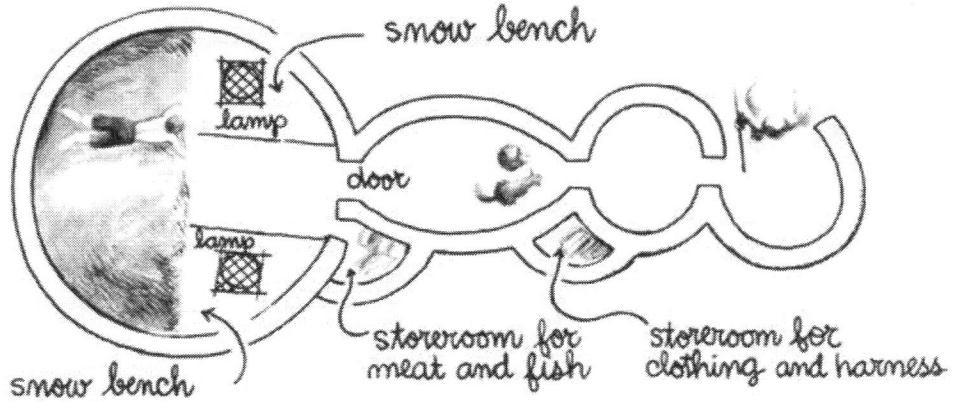

One kind of snow house would look like this if you sawed it from above with the top off.

If you sawed it from the side, it would look like this inside.

Outdoors the sky was sometimes filled with weird, quickly changing colored light, which we call the Aurora Borealis or Northern Lights. This is the way Papik's father explained the lights: Even though people died, their spirits kept on living. Some of them were in the sky. The changing, jumping lights were really spirits having a wonderful time playing a kind of football game—kicking a walrus' head around.

Summer is coming

As the days grew longer, late in winter, Papik and Milak played outdoors more and more. Then one day when Papik climbed on top of the snow house, the roof suddenly caved in! Summer had come. Papik wasn't really surprised. Summer in the Arctic always came in a sudden burst. There was no gradually warming spring.

Nobody scolded Papik for breaking the house. Instead, his family moved into a deerskin tent on the land, where they would live all summer. Dozens and dozens of different kinds of brilliantly colored flowers bloomed in no time. Clouds of mosquitoes appeared and made life uncomfortable for people and dogs. The ocean ice broke up with great cracking noises.

At first the earth was swampy and the Eskimos sometimes starved because they couldn't hunt. As the ground dried out the dogs carried small packs on their backs. The Eskimos had to walk and carry big loads on their own backs, hung from straps around their foreheads.

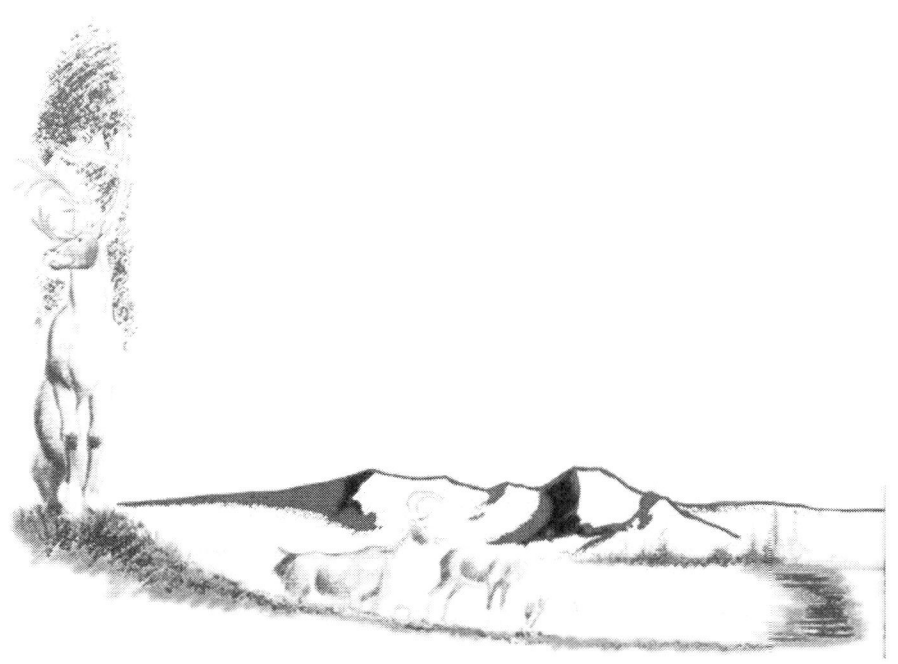

Caribou upon the tundra

As soon as the ice had opened up in the sea and streams and lakes, the Eskimos could travel on water, too. The whole family sometimes got into an umiak—a big boat made of skins. A man or boy could go out in a little skin boat called a kayak.

There was much work to do during the hot days—and plenty of daylight in which to do it. The nights grew shorter, until there was no night at all. The huge sun hung in the sky and never went down. Nobody in the village slept much. Even the children went without any sleep at all for two or three days at a time!

Papik and his father hunted for deer. They used bows shaped from deer antlers and strengthened with deer sinews that had been glued to the horn. Their arrows had points of flint or walrus ivory.

In summer, whales and walruses swam back from warmer water into the Arctic Ocean. To catch them, an Eskimo hunter used a big harpoon. Sometimes he could harpoon a whale from land or from big cakes of ice near land. Often several men went hunting together in an umiak, which had oars and a sail made of seal intestines sewed together. The boat was so light that two men could lift it, but so strong that it could hold two or three tons of whale meat.

Papik hunted these big animals with bow and arrows.

The umiak towed the whale to shore.

Each hunter had his harpoon and line. Tied to the line was a watertight sealskin blown up like a balloon. This was called a float. After the hunters harpooned a whale, the animal tried to swim away, but the floats dragged in the water and finally tired it out. Then it was easy for a man to send a spear straight into the whale's huge heart and kill it.

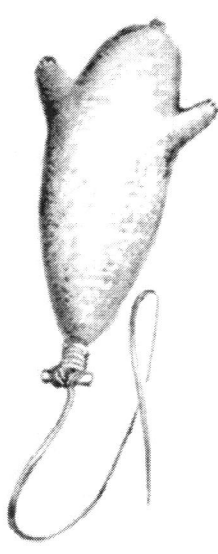

A sealskin float

The whale belonged to the whole village. All the women helped cut it up. And everybody agreed that the best food in the world was the whale's skin and the blubber under it. They cut this off in strips and ate some raw while it was fresh. Then they cut the rest of the whale up and stored it under rocks so that the dogs couldn't get at it.

A drum

After a lucky whaling trip, the villagers naturally wanted to celebrate. So they had a feast. A man beat a big flat drum made of deerskin or sealskin stretched tight over a hoop of wood or bone. People danced and sang songs they made up as they went along. And everybody ate and ate and ate.

In the evening they played catch with a light ball made of skin stuffed with moss. Or they whipped a heavier, clay-stuffed ball around the village with the long whips they used for their dog teams.

A fancy ball

There were other games at feasts, too. The men had archery contests with bows and arrows. When a man hit the target, the women showed their approval by running up and rubbing noses with him.

Men recreate by playing games with balls and whips.

If a strange man came, there was usually a boxing match between him and one of the village men. If the stranger lost, he might have to go away. Life was so hard that only strong people were wanted in an Eskimo village.

Papik practiced these games, just as he practiced hunting. Before long he would be a man and would do the things a man did. There would be a feast when people agreed he was grown up. By then he could take care of himself, even if he was far from any village, all alone in the winter snow.

This is how Eskimos hunted little birds with darts. Each dart had several points.

a throwing board and dart   *a bow drill for making fire*

A throwing board and dart, and a bow drill for making fire.

Eskimos invented ways of killing whales, the largest animals in the world, with only a few pieces of wood and bone and hide. They invented ways of hunting powerful polar bears with only small handmade weapons. They invented a new kind of lamp, which was perfect for their needs.

They made the coldness of the Arctic work for them, when they turned ice and snow into useful tools. They could even make their food do double duty—sometimes they built sleds of frozen skins and meat or fish. Later they and their dogs could have a feast of the thawed-out meat.

Eskimos invented snow goggles to protect their eyes from the glare of sunlight on snow.

Eskimos used every part of an animal. What they didn't eat they turned into clothes or tools or building materials. They even made fine thread from the fibers in bird feathers. All around these two pages you'll find inventions that helped Eskimos to live in the Arctic.

Eskimos invented little skin shoes to protect their dogs' feet when they had to travel over sharp ice.

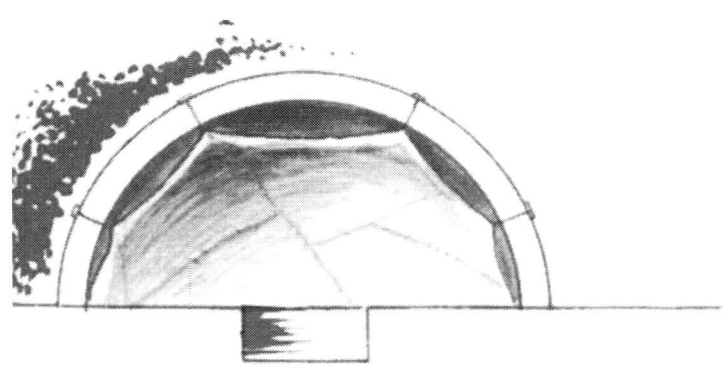

Eskimos often hung skin linings inside their igloo snow houses. This kept the snow from melting and made the house much warmer.

Eskimos fastened waterproof jackets tight to their kayaks. They could turn over in the water without getting anything but their faces and hands wet.

Polar bear

White whale

With fearsome creatures like the polar bear on land and white whale on the sea, the Eskimos had to be clever and inventive to survive.

Eskimos were so good at working with their hands that they could use their wonderful inventions to live alone if they wanted to or had to. But they were very sociable, too. They made lots of visits—and long visits. Nobody ever knocked when he entered a friend's door. In fact, the Eskimos had no word for "Hello." Visitors were expected to come right in.

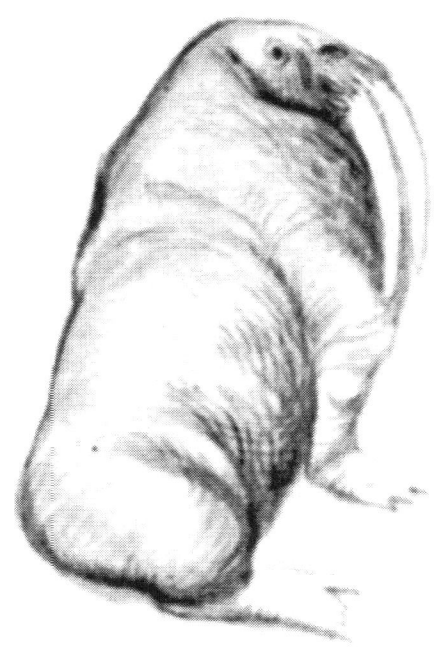

The mighty walrus

As long as there was anything to eat, no Eskimo ever went hungry. Eskimos always shared their food and houses. No one ever owned a house after he moved out of it. But to show that he intended to come back home, he left some tools in his house. Tools, dogs, clothes, good luck charms and toys were about the only things an Eskimo called his own personal property. It never occurred to an Eskimo to pile up wealth enough to hire someone else to work for him.

Narwhal

The Eskimos had no laws about sharing. They knew they must share in order to live at all. They had no chiefs as Indians had, and no police or prisons or warriors.

If people decided something an Eskimo did was wrong, usually they just wouldn't talk to him, or they asked him to leave the village. That was real punishment. Nobody liked a man who was too lazy to hunt, but they divided their food with him and his family anyway. They shared with orphans, too. Every child had a home. Eskimos loved children.

Bowhead whale

The whole village shared the food when these big animals such as these were hunted.

Papik and Milak had never seen a white man. They lived in the days before explorers began to visit the far north country. But other Eskimos had already met white traders and men who hunted whales in sailing vessels.

The village where Hilltop and his sister, Driftwood, lived was near a whaling station at the mouth of the great Mackenzie River in Canada. The children knew some traders and thought they were very funny people indeed. To begin with, white men always had at least two names. No Eskimo ever had more than one, and it was always the name of someone who had died. Eskimos thought that these names were unhappy and brought bad luck unless they were given very soon to a new baby. There were no special girl names, like Mary, or boy names, like John. Any name was good for either a boy or a girl.

Hilltop used a double-ended paddle for his kayak.

White men looked peculiar, too—their beards, for instance. Eskimos almost never had beards, but white men either shaved or had a lot of hair on their faces. White men's beards were a nuisance in winter, because they filled up with icicles and made faces freeze.

Dogs helped hunt bears. The men had to aim their guns carefully. A good dog was worth more than a bearskin.

Even funnier were the traders who had hairy faces but no hair at all on the tops of their heads. Hilltop and Driftwood had never seen a bald Eskimo.

The Eskimos laughed at all the things that seemed so strange and foolish to them. They laughed, too, about the useful things that the white men brought. It was good to light a seal oil lamp with matches instead of a bow-drill. It was safer to kill a polar bear with a gun than with a spear. Now that the Eskimos had guns, hunting was easier, but they had to do more of it. They killed animals for their own use, and they did extra hunting because they needed furs to trade with the white men for bullets and guns and new things to make their homes more comfortable.

Hunters drove caribou into lakes where it was easy to shoot them from kayaks.

This new kind of house was called an igloo, just as snow houses were.

New Ways and Old

Hilltop and Driftwood lived in a house made of logs covered with sod. The sod was grass, dug up with the earth around the roots when the ground wasn't frozen. It helped to keep the houses warm.

Look at the picture and you will see how different this log cabin was from the ones you know about. The walls sloped inward, instead of going straight up. This was important for two reasons. First, piling chunks of sod was easier against sloping walls than against straight ones. Second, the slanting walls made less space at the top. That meant less air to heat than in a squared-off house.

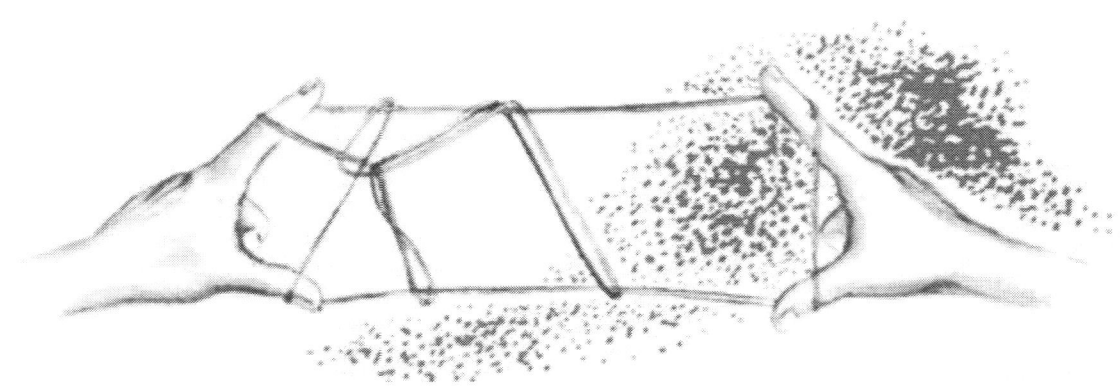

Eskimos played string games like cat's cradle. This one is a deer.

A log house was very warm. In fact, Hilltop and Driftwood felt uncomfortably hot when dinner was being cooked on old-time lamps or over a new-fangled iron stove.

The grownups took off most of their clothes indoors, and the children didn't wear anything. Everybody sweat a great deal. This is how they wiped themselves dry: When the men sat around the house at night, they often spent their time whittling pieces of wood into toys or ornaments or tools. The shavings they made were very small and fine, like excelsior. Piles of the shavings were always heaped up at the side of the room. When anyone got sweaty, he wiped himself dry with the excelsior and threw it away. He used his towel only once, so it never got dirty.

In winter, Hilltop and Driftwood often went traveling with their parents. Riding on sleds, they visited other villages, and sometimes they built snow houses, just as Papik and Milak had done. But their sleds were a little different, and the dogs were not harnessed in the same way. Instead of hitching each dog separately to the sled, Hilltop tied them all to one line and they all pulled together in single file.

Dogs sometimes pulled umiaks on sleds.

Eskimo dogs were tough and strong. Each one knew his own name and the names of all the others in his team. A dog usually hated to leave his team if he was sold. Sometimes he would run away from his new master and travel as much as sixty miles to get back home.

Eskimos took good care of their fierce, hard-working dogs, although they weren't always gentle with them. To train them and make them obey, Eskimos used whips. But they had to be careful. Too much punishment made a dog refuse to work at all. If their dogs hadn't worked and helped them travel, Eskimos couldn't have found enough food and their survival could have been endangered.

Even though Eskimo families traveled far away over wide snowy plains, they never got lost. They knew which way the winds blew, and they could tell by looking at the snowdrifts whether they were keeping on a straight course. In the darkest night they could find their way just by feeling the drifts with their mittened hands.

Sometimes Hilltop went with his father on hunting trips when the ice was breaking up, and he learned about the habits of seals. He learned that a seal is always watching out for polar bears, which are its worst enemy.

When a seal comes out on the ice for a nap, it always chooses an open flat place. That way it can hear bears, or see them, before they come too close. And the seal gets its sleep in little snatches—often only a half-minute nap at a time. Then it wakes up and looks around.

On his first hunting trip, Hilltop saw the seals far off, wiggling and scratching themselves with their flippers. And then he saw his father crouch down and make the same motions! As he crawled along over the ice, he wiggled and scratched. He was making the seal think he was just another seal. Then, when he was close enough, he raised his gun and shot it.

Men often fished this way in spring and autumn. They used their specially made tools to surprise and catch fish in great numbers.

In winter, the men from Hilltop's village also went fishing with nets which they poked down through the ice. Driftwood helped her mother clean the fish with her special woman's knife—the kind that Eskimo women used everywhere. Then she did something many Eskimos never used to do. She cooked the fish.

Once Driftwood tried sprinkling the fish with salt that white traders had given her, but her family didn't like it.

Eskimo women hung fish and meat up to dry like this.

If there were many fish, the women cleaned them, took out the backbones and stored them away to freeze. In early summer and fall, they hung the fish up to dry. Once in a while the men caught so many that the women couldn't keep up with them. Then they cleaned the fish and tossed them into a big box. Later they built a heavy log wall around it to keep out bears and wolves. Hilltop and Driftwood particularly liked to eat this kind of fish raw, after it had been frozen in winter—even if it was rotten.

As summertime came, the whole village waited for the exciting time when the ice began to thaw and break up. The whales and walruses came back into the Arctic Ocean. They swam up between long cracks in the ice called "leads."

Eagerly the men and boys waited along the edges of the leads. Who would see the first walrus? The day Hilltop went with the men in an umiak to hunt whales in a lead was even more exciting. The men paddled a long time before they saw a whale blowing its waterspout in the distance. Then they quickly pulled the umiak out onto the ice and waited.

Suddenly the whale came up to blow again, not far away. The men all fired their guns at once, aiming at its heart, which was deep in its body and as big as a barrel.

A Copper Eskimo bow

It took everybody in the village to pull the whale out onto the ice. They used a block and tackle they had got from the white sailors. Then, after the villagers had cut up the whale, they held a great feast. There was plenty of meat and blubber for all—including the dogs—and whalebone to be traded for more bullets and guns.

Neighbors

Not very far from Hilltop's village lived people that the white men called Copper Eskimos because they had learned to use copper for some of their tools.

Copper Eskimos

A Siberian Eskimo teacher uses books written in the Eskimo language.

Other neighbors along the coast did a new kind of work after white men came. In their high, waterproof boots, they waded into the ocean and chipped away the black rocks near the edge of the water. The rocks were really coal which the white men wanted and taught them to use. Eskimos have always kept on learning how to make the most of the land in which they live.

A Copper Eskimo cache of supplies.

Greenlanders

Nearly half the Eskimos in the world now live in Greenland. Not many of them have ever seen a snow house, although most of their huge island is covered with ice.

With luck a North Greenlander can catch a hundred or more small birds in an hour.

Greenland Eskimos have known white men for more than nine hundred years, but they still hunt in many of the old ways. In the northern part of the island, hunters use nets to catch little birds called auks, which come there by the millions on the exact day the last snow melts in spring. It takes eight or nine auks to make a good meal for one person!

Sometimes Greenlanders paddle their kayaks out to icebergs and perch high up, on the lookout for seals. Instead of being just pure white, the icebergs shine with beautiful tints of blue and green and purple. Greenlanders' clothes, too, are bright, embroidered and decorated with many of the colors of the Aurora Borealis.

People in West Greenland dress like this. Some women pull their hair so tight that it comes out and they often get bald over the ears.

Eskimos are such good mechanics they quickly learned to fit outboard motors on umiaks. This made catching fish much faster for the skilled fishermen of each group.

Trouble Ahead

Traders began to visit the Eskimos in Alaska a long time ago. The Eskimos sold them caribou meat to eat and sealskins—and whalebone. When the traders explained what the whalebone was for, the Eskimos could hardly stop laughing.

Women down in the warm world wanted whalebone to stiffen their corsets, so they would look thin where they weren't. You can imagine how silly this seemed to the Eskimos, who thought people looked best when they were plump all over. But the white men traded them guns and cloth and stoves and tea for whalebone, so they caught many whales.

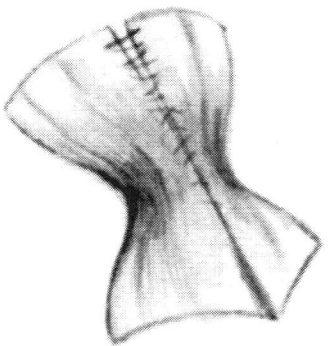

A whalebone corset

For a while the Eskimos got along very well with their trading. Then things changed. Most of the whales had been killed off by white men whose ships could follow the whales all the way as the great sea animals migrated from the Arctic Ocean down toward the South Pole. Most of the walruses were gone, too. The whalers killed them for oil and for their ivory tusks. Next, the caribou began to disappear. Eskimo hunters had killed most of them so that white men could have meat.

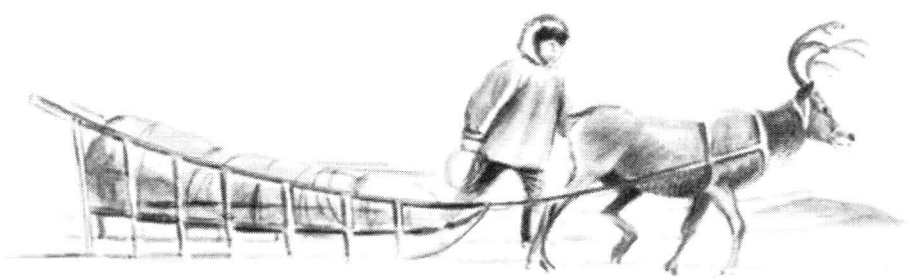

Some Eskimos taught reindeer to pull sleds.

By now, Eskimos had learned to need the things they got from traders, and they were almost starving because so many of their food animals were gone. They needed a new way to make a living. What could they do?

At last the head of the American school for Eskimo children had an idea. He thought of bringing reindeer from Siberia to Alaska. Reindeer are a kind of caribou that has been trained to live with men.

Laplanders from Scandinavia came to teach the Eskimos how to herd reindeer.

He persuaded the government and some individual people to try his plan. The reindeer could eat the grass that grew thick in the hot Alaskan summer. In winter they could use their horns and hoofs to dig down through the thin Arctic snow and eat lichens. A reindeer was a sort of combination horse and cow! It provided meat to eat, milk to drink and strength to pull heavy loads. Its skin was valuable, too.

Alaskan Eskimo children often wear dresses to keep their fur clothes clean.

Reindeer were first brought to Alaska in 1891. Now there are many, many thousands of them.

Eskimo Cowboys

The Alaskan Eskimos became the cowboys of the far north! Each year they have reindeer roundups, much like cattle roundups in the West. Of course, they don't ride horses the way cowboys do. But they sometimes rope reindeers with lariats, and they herd them into huge corrals for branding.

Alaskan kayakers wear waterproof suits made from animal intestines.

The thin reindeer hides are valuable, so Eskimos don't spoil them by burning on a brand. Instead they notch the edges of the animals' ears in special ways. As the reindeer move from the corral through a narrow chute, the cowboys cut the notches, so that each man can tell his own animals.

Very few Eskimos have grown rich from their reindeer, but reindeer herding has become an important way of making a living for some of them. Others still hunt and fish. Some get work part of each year on fishing boats or in mines or on the docks loading ships. But most Eskimos are still very poor.

John and Susie Alook are Eskimo children who live in Alaska today. Although they speak Eskimo at home, they go to school and study English. They learn to read, write and count.

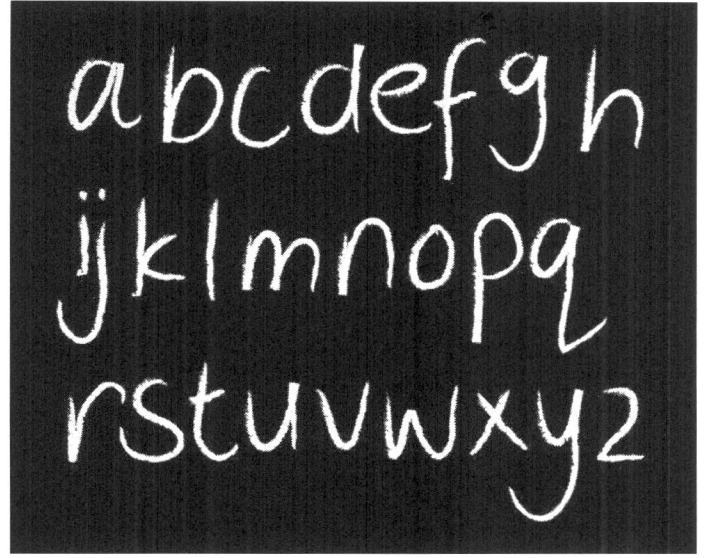

Long ago, when Papik and Milak were children, no Eskimo could count beyond twenty—the number of fingers and toes he had. Any number bigger than that was just "more-than-one-can-count." Some Eskimos only bothered to count to six. That was enough, because they had so few things they needed to count. If they caught a lot of fish, nobody cared to figure out how many. The important thing was that the whole village had enough to eat.

John and Susie Alook have first and last names. Eskimos have borrowed this two-name custom and many others from white people. They have had to learn about doctors and dentists, too, because the Eskimos are not as healthy as they used to be.

Before the white men came, most Eskimos never had decayed teeth. Now they do. Measles, tuberculosis and other diseases which they never had before make them sicker than they make white people. But doctors and nurses are now helping the Eskimos to prevent and cure these new diseases.

When their village has a whale feast, John and Susie share in the celebration and dance, and this is how the dance goes: A lot of people hold a big walrus skin that has hand-holes cut around the edges. John stands on the skin and they toss him into the air.

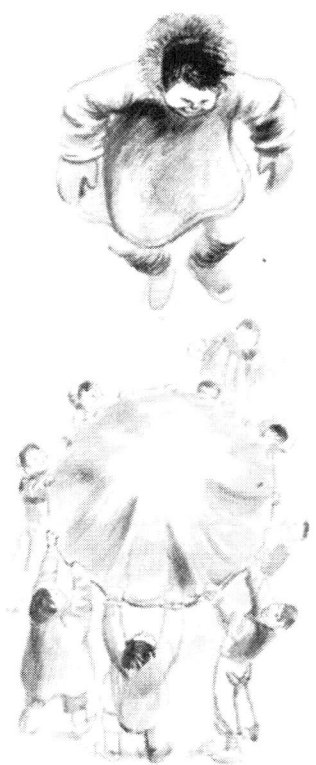

Dancers were sometimes tossed twenty feet up in the air.

Higher and higher they toss him. He keeps his balance, lands on his feet, over and over again, dances in the air and sings a song. At last he tumbles off his feet, and it's someone else's turn. The dancer who goes the highest is the winner.

John and Susie are proud of the way their mother and father can dance—not only the old-time dances but new ones, too. Eskimos are just as good at the white men's dances as the white men are themselves. And they love singing just as much as ever. Now they sing the songs they hear on the radio as well as their own songs.

The new world has brought many changes and many problems to the Eskimos and Inuits. To be sure, they have new inventions, but they have new illnesses, too. Their old way of living is ended, and many are still unsure of whether to cling to the old ways, or embrace the new ones. But they are still The Laughing People.

Made in the USA
Middletown, DE
15 March 2020